This book is dedicated to all the men and women in the world who seek a better quality of life. Lip Scents, Inc. was founded after discovering this priceless book. Lip Scents now takes great joy in sending this gem back to retrieve others big on dreams and low on capital. May this book serve as a treasure map to your own great harvest of unlimited riches.

All the Best-
LeTicia Lee
President & CEO
Lip Scents, Inc.

"Finally, brethren, whatsoever things are true, whatsoever things are honest, whatsoever things are just, whatsoever things are pure, whatsoever things are lovely, whatsoever things are of good report; if there be any virtue, and if there be any praise, think on these things." *Phillipians 4:8*

The S.O. Getting Rich Book

(based on the original 1910 Classic

The Science of Getting Rich)

by

Wallace D. Wattles

Updated and Edited

by

LeTicia Lee

Published by Lulu Press, Inc.

860 Aviation Parkway, Suite 300

Morrisville, NC 27560

ISBN: 978-1-4303 0094-6

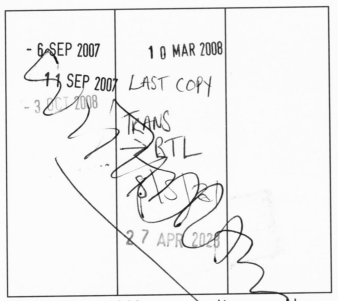
This book should be returned/renewed by
the latest date shown above. Overdue items
incur charges which prevent self-service
renewals. Please contact the library.

Wandsworth Libraries
24 hour Renewal Hotline
01159 293388
www.wandsworth.gov.uk  **Wandsworth**

L.749A (rev.11.2004)

Table of Contents

Preface

This book is pragmatic, not philosophical - a practical manual, not a treatise upon theories. It is intended for the men and women whose most pressing need is for money, who wish to get rich first, and philosophize afterward. It is for those who desire results and who are willing to take the conclusions of science as a basis for action, without going into all the processes by which those conclusions were reached.

It is expected that the reader will take the fundamental statements upon faith, just as he would take statements concerning a law of electrical action if they were revealed by a Marconi or an Edison, and, taking the statements upon faith, that he will prove their truth by acting upon them without fear or hesitation. Every man or woman who does this will certainly get rich, for the science herein applied is an exact science and failure is impossible.

I will cite certain authorities for the benefit of those who wish to investigate philosophical theories (and biblical references) and so secure a logical basis of faith. There is a monistic theory of the universe that One is all and all is One. That One manifests itself as the seeming many elements of the natural world is the foundation of all oriental philosophies. (The Bible sites the same in Romans 12:4-5 and 1 Corinthians 12:27.) Read also the philosophies of Hegel and Emerson for yourself.

I have sacrificed all other considerations to plainness and simplicity of style, so that all might understand. The plan of action laid down herein was deduced from the conclusions of philosophy. It has been thoroughly tested, and bears the supreme test of practical experiment. It works.

The Author

Chapter 1

The Right to Be Rich

Whatever can be said in praise of poverty, the fact remains that it is not possible to live a really complete or successful life unless one is rich. No one can rise to his greatest possible height in talent or soul development unless he has plenty of money. To unfold the soul and to develop talent he must have many things to use, and he cannot have these things unless he has money to buy them.

A person develops in mind, soul, and body by making use of things. Society is now so organized that man must have money in order to become the possessor of things. Therefore, the basis of all advancement must be the science of getting rich.

The object of all life is development. Everything that lives has an inalienable right to all the development it is capable of attaining. A person's right to life means his right to have the free and unrestricted use of all the things which may be necessary to his fullest mental, spiritual, and physical development; or, in other words, his right to be rich.

In this book, I shall not speak of riches in a figurative way. To be really rich does not mean to be satisfied or content with a little. No one ought to be satisfied with a little if he is capable of using and enjoying more. The purpose of nature is the advancement of life. Everyone should have all that can contribute to the power, elegance, beauty, and richness of life. To be content with less is sinful.

The person who owns all he wants for the living of all the life he is capable of living is rich. No person who does not have plenty of money can have all he wants. Life has advanced so far and become so complex that even the most ordinary man or woman requires a great amount of wealth in order to live in a manner that even approaches completeness.

Every person naturally wants to become all that he or she is capable of being. This desire to realize innate possibilities is inherent in human nature. We cannot help wanting to be all that we can be. Success in life is becoming what we want to be. We can become what we want to be only by making use of things, and we can have the free use of things only as we become rich enough to buy them. To understand the science of getting rich is therefore the most essential of all knowledge.

There is nothing wrong with wanting to get rich. The desire for riches is really the desire for a richer, fuller, and more abundant life. That desire is praiseworthy. The person who does not desire to live more abundantly is abnormal. The person who does not desire to have money enough to buy all he wants is abnormal.

There are three motives for which we live. We live for the body. We live for the mind. We live for the soul. No one of these is better or holier than the other. All are alike desirable. No one of the three - body, mind, or soul - can live fully if either of the others is cut short of full life and expression. It is not right or noble to live only for the soul and deny mind or body. It is wrong to live for the intellect and deny body or soul.

We are all acquainted with the loathsome consequences of living for the body and denying both mind and soul. We see that real life means the complete expression of all that a person can give forth through body, mind, and soul. Whatever he can say, no one can be really happy or satisfied

unless his body is living fully in its every function. The same is true of his mind and his soul. Wherever there is unexpressed possibility or function not performed, there is unsatisfied desire. Desire is possibility seeking expression or function seeking performance.

A person cannot live fully in body without good food, comfortable clothing, and warm shelter, and without freedom from excessive toil. Rest and recreation are also necessary to his physical life.

One cannot live fully in mind without books and time to study them, without opportunity for travel and observation, or without intellectual companionship. A person must also have intellectual recreations to develop fully in mind. He must surround himself with all the objects of art and beauty he is capable of using and appreciating.

A person must have love to live fully in soul. Love is denied fullest expression by poverty. A person's highest happiness is found in the bestowal of benefits on those he loves. Love finds its most natural and spontaneous expression in giving. The individual who has nothing to give cannot fill his place as a spouse or parent, as a citizen, or as a human being. It is in the use of material things that a person finds full life for his body, develops his mind, and unfolds his soul. It is therefore of supreme importance for each individual to be rich.

It is perfectly right that you should desire to be rich. If you are a normal man or woman you cannot help doing so. It is perfectly right that you should give your best attention to the science of getting rich, for it is the noblest and most necessary of all studies. If you neglect this study, you are a derelict in your duty to yourself, to God and humanity. You can render to God and humanity no greater service than to make the most of yourself.

Chapter 2

There is a Science

of

Getting Rich

There is a science of getting rich. It is an exact science, like algebra or arithmetic. There are certain laws which govern the process of acquiring riches. Once these laws are learned and obeyed by anyone, that person will get rich with mathematical certainty.

The ownership of money and property comes as a result of doing things in a certain way. Those who do things in this certain way - whether on purpose or accidentally - get rich. Those who do not do things in this certain way - no matter how hard they work or how able they are - remain poor.

It is a natural law that like causes always produce like effects. Therefore, any man or woman who learns to do things in this certain way will infallibly get rich.

That the above statement is true is shown by the following facts: Getting rich is not a matter of environment. If it were, all the people in certain neighborhoods would be wealthy. The people of one city would all be rich, while those of other towns would all be poor. All the inhabitants of one state would roll in wealth, while those of an adjoining state would be in poverty.

Everywhere we see rich and poor living side by side, in the same environment, and often engaged in the same vocations. When two people are in the same locality and in the same business, and one gets rich while the other remains poor, it shows that getting rich is not primarily a matter of environment. Some environments may be more favorable than others, but when two people in the same business are in the same neighborhood and one gets rich while the other fails, it indicates that getting rich is the result of doing things in a certain way.

The ability to do things in this certain way is not due solely to the possession of talent. Many people who have great talent remain poor. Others have very little talent, but get rich.

Studying the people who have gotten rich, we find that they are an average lot in all respects, having no greater talents and abilities than other people. It is evident that they do not get rich because they possess talents and abilities that others do not have. It is because they happen to do things in a certain way.

Getting rich is not the result of saving, or thrift. Many penny pinchers are poor, while free spenders often get rich. (*see Matthew 13:12*)

Getting rich is not due to doing things which others fail to do. Two people in the same business often do almost exactly the same things, and one gets rich while the other remains poor or goes bankrupt.

We must come to the conclusion that getting rich is the result of doing things in a certain way. If getting rich is the result of doing things in a certain way, and if like causes always produce like effects, then any man or woman who can do things in that way can become rich, and the whole matter is brought within the domain of exact science.

The question arises as to whether this certain way may not be so difficult that only a few may follow it. As we have seen, this cannot be true as far as natural ability is concerned. Talented people get rich, and blockheads get rich. Intellectually brilliant people get rich. Very stupid people get rich. Physically strong people get rich, and weak and sickly people get rich.

Some degree of ability to think and understand is essential. However, insofar as natural ability is concerned, any man or woman who has sense enough to read and understand these words can certainly get rich.

Also, we have seen that it is not a matter of environment. Yes, location counts for something. One would not go to the heart of the Sahara Desert and expect to do successful business.

Getting rich involves the necessity of dealing with people and of being where there are people to deal. If these people are inclined to deal in the way you want to deal, so much the better. That is about as far as environment goes. If anyone else in your town can get rich, so can you. If anyone else in your state can get rich, so can you.

Again, it is not a matter of choosing some particular business or profession. People get rich in every business and in every profession, while their next door neighbors in the very same vocation remain in poverty.

It is true that we will do best in a business which we like and which is congenial to us. And if we have certain talents which are well developed, we will do best in a business which calls for the exercise of those talents.

Also, you will do best in a business which is suited to your locality. An ice cream parlor would do better in a warm climate than in the North Pole. A salmon fishery will succeed better in the northwest than in Florida, where there is no salmon.

Aside from these general limitations, getting rich is not dependent upon your engaging in some particular business, but upon your learning to do things in a certain way. If you are now in business and anyone else in your locality is getting rich in the same business, while you are not getting rich, it is simply because you are not doing things in the same way that the other person is doing them.

No one is prevented from getting rich by lack of capital. It is true that as you get capital the increase becomes more easy and rapid. But one who has capital is already rich and does not need to consider how to become so. No matter how poor you may be, if you begin to do things in the certain way you will begin to get rich. You will begin to have capital. The getting of capital is a part of the process of getting rich and it is a part of the result which invariably follows the doing of things in the certain way.

You may be the poorest person on the continent and be deeply in debt. You may have neither friends, influence, nor resources, but if you begin to do things in this way, you must infallibly begin to get rich, for like causes must produce like effects. If you have no capital, you can get capital. If you are in the wrong business, you can get into the right business. If you are in the wrong location, you can go to the right location.

And you can do so by beginning in your present business and in your present location to do things in the certain way which always causes success. You must begin to live in harmony with the laws governing the universe.

Chapter 3

Is

Opportunity

Monopolized?

Nobody is kept poor because other people have monopolized the wealth, and have put a fence around it. We may be shut off from engaging in business in certain lines, but there are other channels open to us.

At different periods the tide of opportunity sets in different directions, according to the needs of the whole and the particular stage of social evolution which has been reached. There is an abundance of opportunity for the person who will go with the tide, instead of trying to swim against it.

Workers, either as individuals or as a class, are not deprived of opportunity. The workers are not being "kept down" by their masters. They are not being "ground" by big business. As a class, they are where they are because they do not do things in a certain way.

The working class may become the master class whenever they will begin to do things in a certain way. The law of wealth is the same for them as it is for all others. This they must learn. They will remain where they are as long as they continue to do as they do. The individual worker, however, is not held down by an entire class's ignorance of these laws. He can follow the tide of opportunity to riches, and this book will tell him how.

No one is kept in poverty by a shortness in the supply of riches. There is more than enough for all.

A palace as large as the capitol at Washington might be built for every family on earth from the building material in the United States alone. Under intensive cultivation this country would produce wool, cotton, linen, and silk enough to clothe each person in the world finer than Solomon was arrayed in all his glory, together with food enough to feed them all luxuriously.

The visible supply is practically inexhaustible. The invisible supply really is inexhaustible.

> *Everything we see on earth is made from One original substance, out of which all things proceed.*

New forms are constantly being made. Older ones are dissolving, but all are shapes assumed by One thing.

There is no limit to the supply of formless stuff, or original substance. The universe is made out of it, but it was not all used in making the universe. The spaces in, through, and between the forms of the visible universe are permeated and filled with the original substance, with the formless stuff - with the raw material of all things. Ten thousand times as much as has been made might still be made, and even then we should not have exhausted the supply of universal raw material.

No person, therefore, is poor because nature is poor or because there is not enough to go around. Nature is an inexhaustible storehouse of riches. The supply will never run short.

> *Original substance is alive with creative energy, and is constantly producing more forms.*

When the supply of building material is exhausted, more will be produced. When the soil is exhausted so that food stuffs and materials for clothing will no longer grow upon it, it will be renewed or more soil will be made. When all the gold and silver has been dug from the earth, if humanity is still in such a stage of social development that it needs gold and silver, more will produced from the Formless. The Formless Stuff responds to the needs of mankind. It will not let the world be without any good thing.

This is true of man collectively. The race as a whole is always abundantly rich. If individuals are poor it is because they do not follow the certain way of doing things which makes the individual rich.

The Formless Stuff is intelligent. It is stuff which thinks. It is alive and is always impelled toward more life. It is the natural and inherent impulse of life to seek to live more. It is the nature of intelligence to enlarge itself, and of consciousness to seek to extend its boundaries and find fuller expression. The universe of forms has been made by formless living substance throwing itself into form in order to express itself more fully.

The universe is a great living presence, always moving inherently toward more life and fuller functioning.

> *Nature is formed for the advancement of life, and its impelling motive is the increase of life. Because of this, everything which can possibly minister to life is bountifully provided. There can be no lack unless God is to contradict himself and nullify His own works.*

We are not kept poor by lack in the supply of riches. It is a fact which I shall demonstrate a little farther on that even the resources of the formless supply are at the command of the man or woman who will act and think in a certain way.

Chapter 4

The First Principle

in the

Science of Getting Rich

Thought is the only power which can produce tangible riches from the formless substance. The stuff from which all things are made is a substance which thinks. Therefore, a thought of form in this substance produces the form.

Original substance moves according to its thoughts. Every form and process we see in nature is the visible expression of a thought in original substance. As the formless stuff thinks of a form, it takes that form. As it thinks of a motion, it makes that motion. That is the way all things were created.

We live in a thought world, which is part of a thought universe. The thought of a moving universe extended throughout formless substance, and the thinking stuff - moving according to that thought - took the form of systems of planets, and maintains that form. Thinking substance takes the form of its thought, and moves according to the thought.

Holding the idea of a circling system of suns and worlds, it takes the form of these bodies, and moves them as it thinks. Thinking the form of a slow-growing oak tree, it moves accordingly. It produces the tree, though centuries may be required to do the work. In creating, the formless seems to move according to the lines of motion it has established. In other words, the thought of an oak tree does not cause the instant formation of a full-grown tree, but it does start in motion the forces which will produce the tree, along established lines of growth.

Every thought of form, held in thinking substance, causes the creation of the form, but most generally, along lines of growth and action already established.

The thought of a house of a certain construction, if it were impressed upon formless substance, might not cause the instant formation of the house, but it would cause the turning of creative energies already working in trade and commerce into such channels as to result in the speedy building of the house. If there were no existing channels through which the creative energy could work, then the house would be formed directly from primal substance, without waiting for the slow processes of the organic and inorganic world. No thought of form can be impressed upon original sub-stance without causing the creation of the form.

A human being is a thinking center and can originate thought. All the forms that a person fashions with his hands must first exist in his thought. *He cannot shape a thing until he has first thought that thing.*

So far humankind has confined its efforts wholly to the work of its hands, applying manual labor to the world of forms and seeking to change or modify those already existing. As yet, few of humankind has thought of trying to cause the creation of new forms by impressing thought upon formless substance.

When a person has a thought-form, he takes material from the forms of nature and makes an image of the form which is in his mind. People have, so far, made little or no effort to cooperate with formless intelligence - to work "with the Father." Few individuals have dreamed of "doing what he sees the Father doing." An individual reshapes and modifies existing forms by manual labor. Most have not given attention to the question of whether they may produce things from formless substance by communicating their thoughts to it.

We propose to prove that human beings may do so. We propose to prove that any man or woman may do so, and to show how. As our first step, we must lay down three fundamental propositions.

First, we assert that there is One original formless stuff or substance from which all things are made. All the seemingly many elements are but different presentations of One element. All the many forms found in organic and inorganic nature are but different shapes, made from the same stuff. And this stuff is thinking stuff.

A thought held in it produces the form of the thought. Thought, in thinking substance, produces shapes. A human being is a thinking center, capable of original thought. If a person can communicate their thought to original thinking substance, that person can cause the creation, or formation, of the thing being thought about.

Summary:

There is a thinking stuff from which all things are made, and which, in its original state, permeates, penetrates, and fills the interspaces of the universe.

A thought in this substance produces the thing that is imaged by the thought.

A person can form things in his thought, and, by impressing thought upon formless substance, can cause the thing thought about to be created.

It may be asked if I can prove these statements, and without going into details I answer that I can do so, both by logic and experience.

Reasoning back from the phenomena of form and thought, we come to one original thinking substance. Reasoning forward from this thinking substance, we come to a person's power to cause the formation of the thing being thought about. And by experiment, we find the reasoning true. This is my strongest proof.

If one person who reads this book gets rich by doing what it tells to do, that is evidence in support of my claim. If every person who does what it tells to do gets rich, that is positive proof until someone goes through the process and fails. The theory is true until the process fails, and this process will not fail. Everyone who does exactly what this book tells to do will get rich.

I have said that people get rich by doing things in a certain way. In order to do so, people must become able to think in a certain way.

A person's way of doing things is the direct result of the way he thinks about things. To do things in the way we want to do them, we have to acquire the ability to think the way we want to think. This is the first step toward getting rich. And to think what we want to think is to think TRUTH, regardless of appearances.

Every individual has the natural and inherent power to think what he wants to think. However, it requires far more effort to do so than it does to think the thoughts which are suggested by appearances.

To think according to appearances is easy. To think truth regardless of appearances is laborious. It requires the expenditure of more power than any other work we are called upon to perform.

There is no labor from which most people shrink as they do from that of sustained and consecutive thought. It is the hardest work in the world. This is especially true when truth is contrary to appearances.

Every appearance in the visible world tends to produce a corresponding form in the mind which observes it. This can only be prevented by holding the thought of the TRUTH.

To look upon the appearances of poverty will produce corresponding forms in your own mind, unless you hold to the truth that there is no poverty. There is only abundance.

To think health when surrounded by the appearances of disease or to think riches when in the midst of the appearances of poverty requires power. Whoever acquires this power becomes a master mind. That person can conquer fate and can have what he wants.

> *This power can only be acquired by getting hold of the basic fact which is behind all appearances, and that fact is that there is One thinking substance from which and by which all things are made.*

Then we must grasp the truth that every thought held in this substance becomes a form. Man can so impress his thoughts upon it as to cause them to take form and become visible things. When we realize this we lose all doubt and fear. We know that we can create what we want to create. We can get what we want to have. We can become what we want to be. As a first step toward getting rich, we must believe the three fundamental statements given previously in this chapter. I will repeat them here for emphasis.

There is a thinking stuff from which all things are made, and in its original state, permeates, penetrates, and fills the interspaces of the universe.

A thought in this substance produces the thing that is imaged by the thought.

—A person can form things in his thought, and by impressing his thought upon formless substance, can cause the thing he thinks about to be created.

You must lay aside all other concepts of the universe. You must dwell upon this until it is fixed in your mind and has become your habitual thought. Read these statements over and over again. Fix every word upon your memory and meditate upon them until you firmly believe what they say. If a doubt comes to you, cast it aside. Do not listen to arguments against this idea. Do not go to churches or lectures where a contrary concept of things is taught or preached. Do not read magazines or books which teach a different idea. If you get mixed up in your understanding, belief, and faith, all your efforts will be in vain.

Do not ask why these things are true nor speculate as to how they can be true. Simply take them on trust. The science of getting rich begins with the absolute acceptance of this.

Chapter 5

Increasing Life

We must get rid of the last vestige of the old idea about a deity whose will it is that anyone should be poor, or whose purposes may be served by keeping anyone in poverty. The intelligent substance which is all, and in all, and which lives in all and lives in you, is a consciously living substance. Being a consciously living substance, it must have the nature and inherent desire of every living intelligence for increase of life. Every living thing must continually seek for the enlargement of its life. Life in the mere act of living, must increase itself.

A seed dropped into the ground springs into activity. In the act of living, it produces a hundred more seeds. Life by living, multiplies itself. It is forever becoming more. It must do so if it continues to be at all.

Intelligence is under this same necessity for continuous increase. Every thought we think makes it necessary for us to think another thought. Consciousness is continually expanding. Every fact learned leads to the learning of another fact. Knowledge is continually increasing. Every talent cultivated brings to consciousness the desire to cultivate another talent. We each are subject to the urge of life, seeking expression, which ever drives us on to know more, do more, and be more.

In order to know more, do more, and be more, we must have more. We must have things to use. We learn, do, and become only by using things. We must be rich so that we can live more.

The desire for riches is simply the capacity for larger life seeking fulfillment. Every desire is the effort of an unexpressed possibility to come into action. It is power seeking to manifest which causes desire. That which makes us desire more money is the same as that which makes the plant grow. It is life seeking fuller expression.

The one living substance must be subject to this inherent law of all life. It is permeated with the desire to live more. That is why it is under the necessity of creating things. The One substance desires to live more in and through us. Therefore it desires us to have all the things we can use.

> *It is the desire of God that we should get rich. God desires us to get rich because God can express better through us if we have plenty of things to use in giving God expression. God can live more in us if we have unlimited command of the means of life.*

The universe desires us to have everything we desire to have a more fulfilling life. Nature is friendly to our plans. Everything is naturally for us. We know that this is true.

It is essential, however, that our purpose should harmonize with the purpose that is in all. We must desire real life, not mere pleasure or sensual gratification. Life is the performance of function. The individual really lives only when he performs every function - physical, mental, and spiritual - of which he is capable, without excess in any.

We must not desire to be rich in order to live greedily. That is not life. We understand that the performance of every physical function is a part of life, and that no one lives completely who denies the impulses of the body a normal and healthful expression.

We must not desire to be rich solely to enjoy mental pleasures, to get knowledge, to gratify ambition, to outshine others, or to be famous. We recognize that all these are a legitimate part of life, but the person who lives for the pleasures of the intellect alone will only have a partial life, and that person will never be satisfied with their lot.

We must not desire to be rich solely for the good of others, to lose ourselves for the salvation of humankind, to experience the joys of philanthropy and sacrifice. The joys of the soul are only a part of life. They are no better or more noble than any other part.

We must desire to be rich in order that we may eat, drink, and be merry when it is time to do these things. We may surround ourselves with beautiful things, see distant lands, feed our minds, and develop our intellect. We may love others and do kind things, and be able to play a good part in helping the world to find truth.

Remember that extreme altruism is no better and no nobler than extreme selfishness. Both are mistakes.

> *Get rid of the idea that God desires us to sacrifice ourselves for others and that we can secure His favor by doing so. God requires nothing of the kind. What God desires is that we should make the most of ourselves, for ourselves, and for others. And we can help others more by making the most of ourselves than in any other way.*

We can make the most of ourselves only by being rich. It is right and praiseworthy that we should give our first and best thought to the work of acquiring wealth.

Remember, however, that the desire of substance is for all, and its movements must be for more life to all. It cannot be made to work for less life to any. It is equally in all, seeking riches and life.

Intelligent substance will make things for us. However, it will not take things away from someone else and give them to us. Get rid of the thought of competition. We are to create, not to compete for what is already created.

You do not have to take anything away from anyone. You do not have to drive sharp bargains. You do not have to cheat or to take advantage. You do not need to let anyone work for less than he earns. You do not have to covet the property of others, or to look at anything with wishful eyes. No one has anything of which you cannot have the like, and you can have such without taking away what another has.

We are creators, not competitors. We will each get what we want in such a way that when we get it, every other person whom we affect will have more than he has now.

I am aware that there are those who get a vast amount of money by proceeding in direct opposition to the statements in the foregoing paragraphs. Therefore, it is wise to add a word of explanation here.

Individuals of that type who become very rich do so sometimes purely by their extraordinary ability on the plane of competition. Sometimes they unconsciously relate themselves to substance in its great purposes and movements for general building through industrial evolution.

Rockefeller, Carnegie, Morgan, et al., were the unconscious agents of the Supreme in the necessary work of systematizing and organizing productive industry. Their work has contributed immensely toward increased life for all, but their day is nearly over.

They organized production and were succeeded by the agents of the multitude, who organized the machinery of distribution. They are like the monster reptiles of the prehistoric eras. They played a necessary part in the evolutionary process; but the same power which produced them, has disposed of them. And it is well to bear in mind that they were never really rich. A record of the private lives of most of this class will show that they were really most abject and wretched.

Riches secured on the competitive plane are never satisfactory and permanent. They are yours today and another's tomorrow. Remember, to become rich in a scientific and certain way, a person must rise entirely out of competitive thought. Never think for a moment that the supply is limited. Just as soon as a person begins to think that all the money is being "cornered" and controlled by others, and that an individual must exert himself to get laws passed to stop this process - in that moment - one is in the competitive mind and the power to cause creation is gone for the time being.

What is worse, the competitive mind arrests the creative movements a person has already begun.

Know that there are countless millions of dollars worth of gold in the mountains of the earth, not yet brought to light. Know that if there were not, more would be created from thinking substance to supply your needs. Know that the money you need will come, even if it is necessary for a thousand men to be led to the discovery of new gold mines tomorrow.

Never look at the visible supply. Look always at the limitless riches in formless substance, and know that all forms of wealth are flowing to you as fast as you can receive and use them. Recognize that nobody by cornering the visible supply, can prevent you from getting what is yours.

— Never allow yourself to think for an instant that all the best building spots will be taken before you get ready to build your house, unless you hurry. Never worry about the major conglomerates and get anxious for fear they will soon come to own the whole earth. Never get afraid that you will lose what you desire because some other person will beat you to it. That cannot possibly happen.

— Do not seek anything that is possessed by anyone else. You are causing what you desire to be created from formless substance, and the supply is without limits. Stick to the formulated statement:

There is a thinking stuff from which all things are made, and which, in its original state, permeates, penetrates, and fills the interspaces of the universe.

— *A thought, in this substance produces the thing that is imaged by the thought.*

— *A person can form things in his thought, and by impressing his thought upon formless substance, can cause the thing thought about to be created.*

Chapter 6

How Riches Come to You

When I said that you do not have to drive sharp bargains, I did not mean that you do not have to drive any bargains at all, or that you are above the necessity for having any dealings with your fellow men. What is meant is that you will not need to deal with others unfairly. You do not have to get something for nothing, but can give to every person more than you take.

We cannot give everyone more in cash market value than we take from them, but we can give more in *use value* than the cash value of the thing we take. The paper, ink, and other material in this book may not be worth the money paid for it, but if the ideas suggested by it bring you thousands of dollars, you have not been wronged by those who sold it to you. They have given you a *greater use value for a small cash value.*

Let us suppose that I own a picture by one of the great artists, which, in a developed society, is worth millions of dollars. If I take it to Antarctica that's inhabited by Eskimos and by "salesmanship" induce a native dweller to give a bundle of furs worth $5,000 for the picture, I have really wronged him. He has no use for the picture. The picture has no use value to him. It will not add to his life.

But suppose I give him several ice fishing rods, and a few dogs to pull his sled worth $300 for his furs. Then he has made a good bargain. He has use for the fishing rods and dogs to help pull his transportation. It will get him more food and add convenience to his travels. It will add to his life in every way. It will make him rich.

When we rise from the competitive to the creative plane, we can scan our business transactions very strictly. If we are selling any person anything which does not add more to his life than the thing he gives us in exchange, we can afford to stop it. You do not have to beat anyone in business. If you are in a business which does beat people, get out of it at once. When we give everyone more in use value than we take from them in cash value, then we are adding to the life of the world by every business transaction.

If you have people working for you, you must take from them more in cash value than you pay them in wages. But you can so organize your business that it will be filled with the principle of advancement. Each employee who wishes to advance can do so a little every day.

You can make your business do for your employees what this book is doing for you. You can so conduct your business that it will be a sort of ladder by which every employee who will take the trouble may climb to riches for themselves. If the person will not do so once given the opportunity, it is not your fault.

Just because you cause the creation of riches from formless substance which permeates all environment, it does not follow that they are to take shape from the atmosphere and come into being before your eyes.

If you desire a personal computer, for instance, I do not mean to tell you that you can impress the thought of a personal computer on thinking substance until the machine is formed without hands, in the room where you sit or elsewhere. But if you desire a personal computer, you can hold the mental image of it with the most positive certainty that it is being made, or is on its way to you. Upon forming the thought, you must have the most absolute and unquestioning faith that the computer is coming. Never think of it or speak of it in any other way than as being sure to arrive. Claim it as yours already.

It will be brought to you by the power of the supreme intelligence, acting upon the minds of men. If you live in Maine, it may be that a person will be brought from Texas or Japan to engage in some transaction which will result in you getting what you want. If so, the whole matter will be as much to that person's advantage as it is to yours.

Do not forget for a moment that the thinking substance is through all, in all, communicating with all, and can influence all. The desire of thinking substance for fuller life and better living has caused the creation of all the personal computers already made, and it can cause the creation of millions more - and will, whenever people set it in motion by desire and faith and by acting in a certain way.

You can certainly have a computer in your home. It is just as certain that you can have any other thing or things which you desire, which will advance your life and the lives of others.

You need not hesitate about asking largely. "It is your Father's pleasure to give you the kingdom," said Jesus. Original substance desires to live all that is possible in you, and desires you to have all that you can use and will use for the living of the most abundant life.

If we fix upon our consciousness on the fact that our desires for the possession of riches is one with the desire of the Supreme Power for more complete expression, our faith becomes invincible.

I once saw a little boy sitting at a piano, vainly trying to bring harmony out of the keys. I saw that he was grieved and provoked by his inability to play real music. I asked him the cause of his vexation, and he answered, "I can feel the music in me, but I can't make my hands go right." The music in him was the URGE of original substance, containing all the possibilities of all life. All that there is of music was seeking expression through the child.

God, the One Substance, is trying to live and do and enjoy things through humanity. He is saying, "I desire hands to build wonderful structures, to play divine harmonies, to paint glorious pictures. I desire feet to run my errands, eyes to see my beauties, tongues to tell mighty truths and to sing marvelous songs," and so on. All that there is of possibility is seeking expression through people. God desires those who can play music to have pianos and every other instrument, and to have the means to cultivate their talents to the fullest extent. He desires those who can appreciate beauty to be able to surround themselves with beautiful things. He desires those who can discern truth to have every opportunity to travel and observe. He desires those who can appreciate dress to be beautifully clothed, and those who can appreciate good food to be luxuriously fed.

He desires all these things because it is Himself that enjoys and appreciates them. They are His creation. It is God who desires to play, sing, enjoy beauty, proclaim truth, wear fine clothes, and eat good foods. The apostle Paul said, "It is God that worketh in me to will and to do."

The desire we feel for riches is the Infinite, seeking to express Himself in us as He sought to find expression in the little boy at the piano. So we need not hesitate to ask largely. Our part is to focus on and express that desire to God.

This is a difficult point with most people. They retain something of the old idea that poverty and self-sacrifice are pleasing to God. They look upon poverty as a part of the plan, a necessity of nature.

They have the idea that God has finished his work, and made all that He can make, and that the majority of people must stay poor because there is not enough to go around. They hold to so much of this erroneous thought that they feel ashamed to ask for wealth. They try not to want more than a very modest competence, just enough to make them fairly comfortable.

I recall the case of one student who was told that he must get in mind a clear picture of the things he desired, so that the creative thought of them might be impressed on formless substance. He was a very poor man, living in a rented house and having only what he earned from day to day, and he could not grasp the fact that all wealth was his. After thinking the matter over, he decided that he might reasonably ask for a new rug for the floor of his best room and a coal stove to heat the house during the cold weather. Following the instructions given in this book, he obtained these things in a few months.

And then it dawned upon him that he had not asked enough. He went through the house in which he lived, and planned all the improvements he would like to make in it. He mentally added a bay window here and a room there, until it was complete in his mind as his ideal home. He then planned its furnishings.

Holding the whole picture in his mind, he began living in the certain way and moving toward what he desired. He now owns the house and is rebuilding it after the form of his mental image. Now, with still larger faith, he is going on to obtain even greater things. It has been unto him according to his faith, and so it is with you - and with all of us.

Chapter 7

Gratitude

The illustrations given in the last chapter will have conveyed to the reader the fact that the first step toward getting rich is to convey the idea of our desires to the formless substance. This being true, then we must see that in order to do so, it becomes necessary to relate ourselves to the formless intelligence in a harmonious way.

To secure this harmonious relation is a matter of such primary and vital importance that I will give some space to its discussion here and give instructions which, if the reader will follow them, will be certain to bring him into perfect unity of mind with the supreme power, a.k.a God.

The whole process of mental adjustment and attunement can be summed up in one word: Gratitude.

First, we believe that there is One intelligent substance, from which all things proceed.

Second, we believe that this Substance gives us everything we desire.

Third, we relate ourselves to It by a feeling of deep and profound gratitude.

Many people who order their lives rightly in all other ways are kept in poverty by their lack of gratitude. Having received one gift from God, they cut the wires which connect them with Him by failing to make acknowledgment.

It is easy to understand that the nearer we live to the Source of wealth, the more wealth we shall receive. And it is easy also to understand that the soul that is always grateful lives in closer touch with God than the one which never looks to God in thankful acknowledgment.

The more gratefully we fix our minds on the Supreme when good things come to us, the more good things we will receive, and the more rapidly they will come. The reason is simply that the mental attitude of gratitude draws the mind into closer touch with the Source from which the blessings come.

If it is a new thought to you that gratitude brings your whole mind into closer harmony with the creative energies of the universe, consider it well. The good things that have come to you already, have done so along the line of obedience to certain laws. Gratitude will lead your mind out along the ways by which things come. It will keep you in close harmony with creative thought, and prevent you from falling into competitive thought.

Gratitude alone can keep you looking toward the all, and prevent you from falling into the error of thinking of the supply as limited. To do that would be fatal to your hopes. There is a law of gratitude, and it is absolutely necessary that you should observe the law if you are to get the results you seek. The law of gratitude is the natural principle that action and reaction are always equal and in opposite directions.

The grateful outreaching of mind in thankful praise to the Supreme Intelligence is a liberation or expenditure of force. It cannot fail to reach that to which it is addressed, and the reaction is an instantaneous movement toward you.

"Draw nigh unto God, and He will draw nigh unto you." That is a statement of psychological truth. And if your gratitude is strong and constant, the reaction in formless substance will be strong and continuous. The movement of the things you desire will be always toward you. Notice the grateful attitude that Jesus took, how he always seemed to be saying, "Father, I thank Thee that thou hast heard me." We cannot exercise much power without gratitude, for it is gratitude that keeps us connected with the Source of power.

The value of gratitude does not consist solely in getting us more blessings in the future. Without gratitude we cannot long keep from dissatisfied thought regarding things as they are.

The moment we permit our mind to dwell with dissatisfaction upon things as they are, we begin to lose ground. If we fix our attention upon the common, the ordinary, the poor, the squalid, and the mean - then our mind takes the form of these things. Then we transmit these forms or mental images to the Formless. And the common, the poor, the squalid, and the mean would come to us. To permit your mind to dwell upon the inferior is to become inferior and to surround yourself with inferior things.

On the other hand, to fix your attention on the best is to surround yourself with the best, and to become the best. The creative power within us makes us into the image of that to which we give our attention. We are of thinking substance, and thinking substance always takes the form of that which it thinks about.

The grateful mind is constantly fixed upon the best. Therefore it tends to become the best. It takes the form or character of the best, and will receive the best.

Also, faith is born of gratitude. The grateful mind continually expects good things, and expectation becomes faith. The reaction of gratitude upon one's own mind produces faith, and every outgoing wave of grateful thanksgiving increases faith. The person who has no feeling of gratitude cannot long retain a living faith, and without a living faith you cannot get rich by the creative method, as we shall see in the following chapters.

It is necessary, then, to cultivate the habit of being grateful for every good thing that comes to us and to give thanks continuously. Because all things have contributed to your advancement, you should include all things in your gratitude.

Do not waste a lot of time thinking or talking about the shortcomings or wrong actions of those in power. Their organization of the world has created your opportunity. All we get really comes to us because of them. Do not rage against corrupt politicians. If it were not for politicians we would fall into anarchy and opportunities would be greatly lessened.

God has worked a long time and very patiently to bring us up to where we are in industry and government, and He is going right on with His work. There is not the least doubt that He will do away with plutocrats, trust magnates, captains of industry, and politicians as soon as they can be spared, but in the meantime, they are all very necessary. Remember, they are all helping to arrange the lines of transmission along which your riches will come to you. Be grateful. This will bring you into harmonious relations with the good in everything, and the good in everything will move toward you.

Chapter 8

Thinking
in
the Certain Way

Turn back to Chapter 6 and read again the story of the man who formed a mental image of his house to get a fair idea of the initial step toward getting rich. We must form a clear and definite mental picture of what we desire. We cannot transmit an idea unless we have it ourselves.

We must have it before we can give it. Many people fail to impress thinking substance because they have themselves only a vague and misty concept of the things they desire to do, have, or become.

It is not enough that you should have a general desire for wealth to do good. Everyone has that desire. It is not enough that you should have a wish to travel, see things, live more, etc. Everyone has those desires too. If you were going to send a wireless message to a friend, you would not send the letters of the alphabet in their order and let him construct the message for himself, nor would you take words at random from the dictionary. You would send a coherent sentence, one which meant something.

When impressing desires upon the thinking substance, remember that it must be done by a coherent statement. You must know what you want and be specific and definite. You can never get rich or start the creative power into action by sending out unformed longings and vague desires.

You must go over your desires just as the man described went over his house. You must see just what you desire, and get a clear mental picture of it as you wish it to look when you get it.

You must continually have that clear mental picture in mind. Just as the pilot has in mind the destination toward which he is flying his aircraft, you must keep your face toward it all the time. You must no more lose sight of it than the pilot loses sight of the compass to keep him going in the right direction.

It is not necessary to take exercises in concentration, nor to set apart special times for prayer and affirmation, nor to "go into the silence," nor to do occult stunts of any kind. Some of these things are well enough, but you need only to know what you want and to desire it strongly enough so that it will stay in your thoughts.

Spend as much of your leisure time as you can in contemplating your picture. Realize that no one needs to take exercises to concentrate their mind on a thing which is really desired. It is the things we do not really care about which requires effort not to fix your attention upon them.

Unless you really want to get rich, so that the desire is strong enough to hold your thoughts directed to the purpose as the magnetic pole holds the needle of the compass, it will hardly be worth-while for you to try to carry out the instructions given in this book.

The methods set forth here are for people whose desire for riches is strong enough to overcome mental laziness and the love of ease, and to make them work.

The more clear and definite you make your picture, and the more you dwell upon it, bringing out all its delightful details, the stronger your desire will be. The stronger your desire, the easier it will be to hold your mind fixed upon the picture of what you desire.

Something more is necessary, however, than merely to see the picture clearly. If that is all you do, you are only a dreamer, and will have little or no power for accomplishment. Behind your clear vision must be the purpose to realize it, to bring it out in tangible expression. And behind this purpose must be an invincible and unwavering FAITH that the thing is already yours, that it is — "at hand" and you have only to take possession of it.

Live in the new house, mentally, until it takes form around — you physically. In the mental realm, enter at once into full enjoyment of the things you desire.

"Whatsoever things ye ask for when ye pray, believe that ye receive them, and ye shall have them," said Jesus.

See the things you desire as if they were actually around you all the time. See yourself as owning and using them. Make use of them in imagination just as you will use them when they are your tangible possessions. Dwell upon your mental picture until it is clear and distinct, and then take the mental attitude of ownership toward everything in that picture. Take possession of it, in mind, in the full faith that it is actually yours. Hold to this mental ownership. Do not waiver for an instant in the faith that it is real.

Remember what was said in a proceeding chapter about gratitude. Be as thankful for it all the time as you expect to be when it has taken form. The person who can sincerely thank God for the things which he owns only in imagination has real faith. That person will get rich, and will cause the creation of whatever is desired.

You do not need to pray repeatedly for things you desire. It is not necessary to tell God about it every day.

Your part is to intelligently formulate your desire for the things which make for a larger life and to get these desires arranged into a coherent whole. Then, impress this whole desire upon Formless Substance, which has the power and the will to bring you what you desire.

You do not make this impression by repeating strings of words. You make it by holding the vision with unshakable PURPOSE to attain it and with steadfast FAITH that you do attain it. The answer to prayer is not according to your faith while you are talking, but according to your faith while you are working.

We cannot impress God by having a special Sabbath day set apart to tell Him what we desire, and then forget Him during the rest of the week. We cannot impress Him by having special hours to go into our closet and pray, if we then dismiss the matter from our minds until the hour of prayer comes again.

Oral prayer is well enough, and has its effect, especially upon ourselves. It helps us to clarify our vision and strengthen our faith. But it is not our oral petitions alone which get us what we want. In order to get rich we do not need a sweet hour of prayer; we need to pray without ceasing. And by prayer, I mean holding steadily to your vision, with the purpose to cause its creation into solid form, and the faith that you are doing so.

Once you have clearly formed your vision, the whole matter turns on receiving. When you have formed it, it is well to make an oral statement, addressing the Supreme in gratitude. Then, from that moment on you must, in mind, receive that which you asked.

Live in the new house. Wear the fine clothes. Ride in the new automobile. Go on the journey, and confidently plan for greater journeys. Think and speak of all the things you have asked for in terms of actual present ownership. Imagine an environment and a financial condition exactly as you desire them. Live all the time in that mental environment and financial condition until they take physical shape.

Mind, however, that you do not do this as a mere dreamer and castle builder. Hold to the FAITH that the imaginary is being realized, and to your PURPOSE to realize it. Remember that it is faith and purpose in the use of the imagination which make the difference between the scientist and the dreamer. Having learned this fact, it is here that we must learn the proper use of the will.

Chapter 9

How to Use the Will

You do not attempt to apply your will power to anything outside of yourself when getting rich in a scientific way. You have no right to do so. It is wrong to apply your will to other men and women in order to get them to do what you wish done.

It is just as wrong to coerce people by mental power as it is to coerce them by physical power. If compelling people by physical force to do things reduces them to slavery, then compelling them by mental means accomplishes exactly the same thing. The only difference is in methods. If taking things from people by physical force is robbery, them taking things by mental force is robbery also. There is no difference in principle.

We have no right to use our will power upon another person, even presuming it is "for their own good," for we do not know what is for their good. The science of getting rich does not require us to apply power or force to any other person, in any way whatsoever. There is not the slightest necessity for doing so. Any attempt to use our will upon others will only tend to defeat our purpose.

We do not need to apply our will to things in order to compel them to come to us. That would simply be trying to coerce God and would be foolish and useless. We do not have to try to compel God to give us good things, any more than we have to use our will power to make the sun rise.

We do not have to use our will power to conquer an unfriendly deity, or to make stubborn and rebellious forces do our bidding. Substance is friendly to us. It is more anxious to give us what we desire than we are to get it. We need only to use our will power upon ourselves to get rich.

When you know what to think and do, then you must use your will to compel yourself to think and do the right things. That is the legitimate use of the will in getting what you want. Use it to hold yourself on the right course. Use the will to keep yourself thinking and acting in the certain way.

Do not attempt to project your will, your thoughts, or your mind out into space to "act" on things or people. Keep your mind at home. You can accomplish more there than elsewhere.

Use your mind to form a clear mental image of what you want. Hold that vision with faith and purpose. Use your will to keep your mind working in the *right* way.

The more steady and continuous your faith and purpose, the more rapidly you will get rich. You will stay rich, because you will make only POSITIVE impressions upon Substance. Do not neutralize or offset them with negative impressions.

The picture of your desires, held with faith and purpose, is taken up by the formless. This clear mental image permeates to great distances - throughout the universe, for all we know.

As this impression spreads, all things are set in motion towards its realization. Every living thing is stirred toward bringing into being that which you desire. All force begins to exert itself in that direction. All things begin to move towards you. The minds of people everywhere are influenced towards doing the things necessary to fulfill your desires. Living forces begin to work for you, unconsciously.

However, you can check all this by starting a negative impression in the formless substance. Doubt or unbelief is as certain to start a movement away from you as faith and purpose are to start one towards you. It is by not understanding this that most people make their failure. Every hour and moment you spend in giving heed to doubts and fears, every hour you spend in worry, every hour in which your soul is possessed by unbelief, sets a current away from you in the whole domain of Intelligent Substance. All the promises are unto them that believe, and unto them only.

Since belief is all important, it behooves us to guard our thoughts. And as our beliefs are shaped to a very great extent by the things we observe and think about, it is important to carefully govern to what we give our attention.

Here the will comes into use. It is your will that determines what things your attention shall be fixed.

If you desire to be rich, you must not make a study of poverty. Things are not brought into being by thinking about their opposites. Health is never to be attained by studying disease and thinking about disease. Righteousness is not to be promoted by studying sin and thinking about sin. No one ever got rich by studying poverty and thinking about poverty.

Medicine as a science of disease has increased disease. Religion as a science of sin has promoted sin. Economics as a study of poverty will fill the world with wretchedness and desire for evil. Do not talk about poverty. Do not investigate it, or concern yourself with it. Never mind what its causes are; have nothing to do with them. What concerns us is the cure.

Do not spend time in so-called charitable work or charity movements. Most charity only tends to perpetuate the wretchedness it aims to eradicate. I do not say that you should be hard-hearted or unkind and refuse to hear the cry of need, but you must not try to eradicate poverty in any of the conventional ways. Put poverty behind you, and put all that pertains to it behind you, and "make good." Get rich. That is the best way you can help the poor.

We cannot hold the mental image which is to make us rich if we fill our minds with pictures of poverty and all its attendant ills. Do not read books or papers which give circumstantial accounts of the wretchedness of the tenement dwellers, of the horrors of child labor, and so on. Do not read anything which fills the brain with gloomy images of want and suffering. You cannot help the poor in the least by knowing about these things, and the wide-spread knowledge of them does not tend at all to do away with poverty.

What tends to do away with poverty is not the getting of pictures of poverty into your mind, but getting pictures of wealth, abundance, and possibility into the minds of the poor. We are not deserting the poor in their misery when we refuse to allow our minds to be filled with pictures of that misery.

Poverty can be done away with, not by increasing the number of well-to-do people who think about poverty, but by increasing the number of poor people whose purpose with faith attain to get rich.

The poor do not need charity; they need inspiration. Charity only sends them a loaf of bread to keep them alive in their wretchedness, or gives them an entertainment to make them forget for an hour or two. *But inspiration can cause them to rise out of their misery.* If you desire to help the poor, demonstrate to them that they can become rich. Prove it by getting rich yourself.

The only way in which poverty will ever be banished from this world is by getting a large and constantly increasing number of people to practice the teachings of this book. People must be inspired to learn to become rich by creation, not by competition.

Every person who becomes rich by competition knocks down the ladder by which he rises, and keeps others down. Every person who gets rich by creation opens a way for thousands to follow, and inspires them to do so.

You are not showing hardness of heart or an unfeeling disposition when you refuse to pity poverty, see poverty, read about poverty, think or talk about it, or to listen to those who do talk about it. Use your will power to keep your mind OFF the subject of poverty and to keep it fixed with faith and purpose ON the vision of what you desire and are creating.

Chapter 10

Further Use of the Will

We cannot retain a true and clear vision of any form of wealth if we are constantly turning our attention to opposing pictures, whether they be external or imaginary. Put poverty and all things that pertain to poverty completely behind you. Do not tell of your past troubles of a financial nature, if you have had them. Do not think of them at all. Do not tell of the poverty of your parents, or the hardships of your early life. To do any of these things is to mentally class yourself with the poor for the time being, and it will certainly check the movement of those things in your direction.

We have accepted a certain theory of the universe as being correct, and rest all our hopes of happiness on its being correct. What can you gain by giving heed to conflicting theories?

Do not read books which tell you that the world is soon coming to an end. Do not read the writings of pessimistic philosophers who tell you that it is going to the devil. The world is not going to the devil; it is going to God. It is a wonderful becoming.

True, there may be a good many things in current conditions which are disagreeable, but what is the use of studying them when they are certainly passing away. The study of them only tends to slow their passing and keep them with us. Why give time and attention to things which are being removed by evolutionary growth? We can hasten their removal only by promoting the evolutionary growth as far as our part of it goes.

No matter how horrible the conditions may seem to be in certain countries, sections, or places, by dwelling on them, we waste our time and destroy our own chances. Interest yourself in the world's becoming rich.

Think of the riches the world is manifesting, instead of the poverty it is leaving behind. Bear in mind that the only way in which we can assist the world in growing rich is by growing rich ourselves through the creative method, not the competitive one.

Give your attention wholly to riches. Do not focus on poverty. Whenever you think or speak of those who are poor, think and speak of them as those who are becoming rich, as those who are to be congratulated rather than pitied. They and others will catch the inspiration, and begin to search for the way out.

Because we say that you are to give your whole time and mind and thought to riches, it does not follow that you are to be sordid or mean. Becoming rich is the noblest aim you can have in life, for it includes everything else. (See Bible reference 3 John 2)

On the competitive plane, the struggle to get rich is a godless scramble for power over others. When we come into the creative mind, all this is changed. All that is possible in the way of greatness, of service and lofty endeavor, comes by way of getting rich, because all is made possible by the use of things.

You can aim at nothing so great or noble, I repeat, as to become rich. You must fix your attention upon the mental picture of wealth to the exclusion of all that may tend to dim or obscure the vision.

Some people remain in poverty because they are ignorant of the fact that there is wealth for them. These facts can best be inspired to be learned by showing them the way to affluence in your own person and practice.

Others are poor because, while they feel that there is a way out, they are too intellectually indolent to put forth the mental effort necessary to find that way and travel it. For these, the very best thing you can do is to arouse their desire by showing them the happiness that comes from being *rightly rich.*

Still others are poor, because while they have some notion of science, they have become so swamped and lost in the maze of theories that they do not know which road to take. They try a mixture of many systems and fail in all. For these, again, the very best thing to do is to show the right way in your own person and practice. An ounce of doing things is worth a pound of theorizing.

> *The very best thing you can do for the whole world is to make the most of yourself. You can serve God and humanity in no more effective way than by being rich; that is, if you get rich by the creative method and not by the competitive one.*

I assert that this book gives in detail the principles of the science of getting, and if that is true, the practitioner needs to read no other book upon the subject. This may sound narrow and egotistical. However, consider this. There is no more scientific method of computation in mathematics than by addition, subtraction, multiplication, and division. No other method is possible. There can be but one shortest distance between two points. There is only one way to think scientifically, and that is to think in the way that leads by the most direct and simple route to the goal. No one has yet formulated a briefer or less complex "system" than the one set forth here. It has been stripped of all non-essentials. When you commence on this, lay all others aside. Put them out of your mind altogether.

Read this book every day. Keep it with you. Commit it to memory. Do not think about other systems and theories. If you do, you will begin to have doubts and to be uncertain and wavering in your thought. Then you will begin to make failures. After you have made good and become rich, you may study other systems as much as you please.

Read only the most optimistic comments on the world's news. Read those in harmony with your picture. Do not dabble in spiritualism, or kindred studies. Perhaps the dead still live and are near, but if they are, let them alone. Mind your own business. Wherever the spirits of the dead may be, they have their own work to do. We have no right to interfere with them. We cannot help them. It is very doubtful whether they can help us, or whether we have any right to trespass upon their time if they can. Let the dead and the hereafter alone. Solve your own problem. Get rich. If you begin to mix with the occult, you will start mental cross-currents which will surely bring your hopes to wreck.

Now, this and the preceding chapters have brought us to the following statement of basic facts:

There is a thinking stuff from which all things are made, and which, in its original state, permeates, penetrates, and fills the interspaces of the universe.

— *A thought in this substance produces the thing that is imaged by the thought.*

— *A person can form things in his thought, and, by impressing his thought upon formless substance, can cause the thing he thinks about to be created.*

— *In order to do this, a person must pass from the competitive to the creative mind. He must form a clear mental picture of the things he desires, and hold this picture in his thoughts with the fixed PURPOSE to get what he wants, and the unwavering FAITH that he does get what he wants. He closes his mind against all that may tend to shake his purpose, dim his vision, or quench his faith.*

In addition to this, we shall now see that we must live and act in a certain way.

Chapter 11

Acting
in
The Certain Way

Thought is the impelling force, which causes the creative power to act. Thinking in a certain way will bring riches to you. However, you must not rely upon thought alone, paying no attention to personal action. That is the rock upon which many otherwise scientific thinkers meet havoc. They fail to connect thought with personal action.

We have not yet reached the stage of development, even supposing such a stage to be possible, in which a person can create directly from formless substance without nature's processes or the work of human hands. We must not only think; our personal action must supplement our thought.

By thought we can cause the gold in the hearts of the mountains to be impelled toward us. However, it will not mine itself, refine itself, coin itself into double eagles, and come rolling along the roads, seeking its way into our pockets.

Under the impelling power of Supreme Spirit, people's affairs will be so ordered that someone will be led to mine the gold for you. Other people's business transactions will be so directed that the gold will be brought toward you.

We must so arrange our own business affairs that we may be able to receive it when it comes to us. Our thoughts make all things, animate and inanimate, work to bring us what we desire; but our personal activity must be such that we can rightly receive what we desire when it reaches us. We are not to take it as charity, nor to steal it. We must give every person more in use value than is given us in cash value.

The scientific use of thought consists in forming a clear and distinct mental image of what we want, in holding fast to our purpose to get what we want, and in realizing with grateful faith that we do get what we want.

Do not try to project your thought in any mysterious or occult way, with the idea of having it go out and do things for you. That is wasted effort and will weaken your power to think with sanity.

The action of thought in getting rich is fully explained in the preceding chapters. Your faith and purpose positively impress your vision upon formless substance, which has the same desire for more life that you have. This vision, received from you, sets all the creative forces at work in and through their regular channels of action, but directed towards you.

It is not our part to guide or supervise the creative process. All we have to do with that is to retain our vision, stick to our purpose, and maintain our faith and gratitude.

We must act in a certain way, so that we can appropriate what is ours when it comes to us. We can meet the things we have in our picture and put them in their proper places as they arrive.

You can really see the truth of this. When things reach you, they will be in the hands of others. They will ask an equivalent in exchange for them. You can only get what is yours by giving the other person what is rightfully his.

Your pocketbook is not going to be transformed into a Fortunata's purse, which shall be always full of money without effort on your part.

This is the crucial point in the science of getting rich - right here, where thought and personal action must be combined.

There are very many people who, consciously or unconsciously, set the creative forces in action by the strength and persistence of their desires. They remain poor because they do not provide for the reception of the thing they desire when it comes.

> *By thought, the thing we want is brought to us. By action, we receive it.*
>
> *Whatever your action is to be, it is evident that you must act NOW. You cannot act in the past. It is essential to the clearness of your mental vision that you dismiss the past from your mind. You cannot act in the future, for the future is not here yet. You cannot tell how you will want to act in any future contingency until that contingency has arrived.*

Because you are not in the right business or the right environment, do not think that you must postpone action until you get into the right business or environment. Do not spend time in the present, taking thought as to the best course in possible future emergencies. Have faith in your ability to meet any emergency when it arrives.

If you act in the present with your mind on the future, your present action will be with a divided mind, and will not be effective. Put your whole mind into present action.

Do not give creative impulse to original substance, and then sit down and wait for results. If you do, you will never get them. Act now. There is never any time but now, and there never will be any time but now. If you are ever to begin to make ready for the reception of what you desire, you must begin NOW. Your action, whatever it is, must most likely be in your present business or employment, and must be upon the persons and things in your present environment.

You cannot act where you are not. You cannot act where you have been. You cannot act where you are going to be. You can only act where you are.

Do not bother as to whether yesterday's work was well done or ill done. Do today's work well. Do not try to do tomorrow's work now. There will be plenty of time to do that when you get to it.

Do not try, by occult or mystical means, to act on people or things that are out of your reach. Do not wait for a change of environment, before acting. Get a change of environment by action. You can so act upon the environment in which you are, as to cause yourself to be transferred to a better environment. Hold with faith and purpose the vision of yourself in the better environment, but act in your present environment with all your heart, all your strength, and all your mind.

Do not spend any time day dreaming or castle building. Hold to the one vision of what you want, and act NOW.

Do not cast about, seeking some new thing to do or some strange, unusual, or remarkable action to perform as a first step toward getting rich. It is probable that your actions, at least for some time, will be the same ones you have been performing for some time past, but you can begin now to perform these actions in the certain way, which will surely make you rich.

If you are engaged in some business, and feel that it is not the right one for you, do not wait until you get into the right business before you begin to act.

Do not feel discouraged or sit down and lament because you are misplaced. No one is so misplaced that he cannot find the right place, and no one is so involved in the wrong business that he cannot get into the right business.

Hold the vision of yourself in the right business, with the purpose to get into it. Hold it with faith that you will get into it and are getting into it, but ACT in your present business.

Use your present business as the means of getting into a better one. Use your present environment as the means of getting into a better one. Your vision of the right business, if held with faith and purpose, will cause the Supreme Power to move the right business towards you. Your action, if performed in the certain way, will cause you to move towards that business.

If you are an employee and feel that you must change places in order to get what you want, do not project your thought into space and rely upon it to get you another job. It will probably fail to do so.

Hold the vision of yourself in the job you desire while you ACT with faith and purpose on the job you have. You will certainly get the job you want.

Your vision and faith will set the creative force in motion to bring it towards you. Your action will cause the forces in your own environment to move you towards the place you desire. In closing this chapter, we will add another statement to our syllabus:

There is a thinking stuff from which all things are made, and which, in its original state, permeates, penetrates, and fills the interspaces of the universe.

A thought in this substance produces the thing that is imaged by the thought.

A person can form things in his thought, and, by impressing his thought upon formless substance, can cause the thing thought about to be created.

In order to do this, a person must pass from the competitive to the creative mind. He must form a clear mental picture of the things he desires, and hold this picture in his thoughts with the fixed PURPOSE to get what he wants, and the unwavering FAITH that he does get what he wants, closing his mind to all that may tend to shake his purpose, dim his vision, or quench his faith.

So that he may receive what he wants when it comes, a person must act NOW upon the people and things in his present environment.

Chapter 12

Efficient Action

You must use your thought as directed in previous chapters and begin to do what you can where you are. Do all that you can do where you are now.

You can only advance by being larger than your present place. No one is larger than his present place who leaves undone any of the work pertaining to that place. The world is advanced only by those who more than fill their present places.

If no one quite filled his present place, you can see that there must be a going backward in everything. Those who do not quite fill their present places are dead weight upon society. They must be carried along by others at a great expense. The progress of the world is slowed only by those who do not fill the places they are holding. They belong to a former age and their tendency is toward degeneration. No society could advance if everyone was smaller than his place. Social evolution is guided by the law of physical and mental evolution.

In the animal world, evolution is caused by excess of life. When an organism has more life than can be expressed in the functions of its own plane, it develops the organs of a higher plane, and a new species is originated.

There never would have been new species had there not been organisms which more than filled their places. The law is exactly the same for us. Getting rich depends upon us applying this principle to our own affairs.

Every day is either a successful day or a day of failure. It is the successful days which get you what you want. If every day is a failure you can never get rich. If every day is a success, you cannot fail to get rich. If there is something that may be done today and you do not do it, you have failed insofar as that thing is concerned - and the consequences may be more disastrous than you imagine.

We cannot foresee the results of even the most trivial act. We do not know the workings of all the forces that have been set moving in our behalf. Much may be depending on us doing some simple act, and it may be the very thing which is to open the door of opportunity to very great possibilities. We can never know all the combinations which Supreme Intelligence is making for us in the world of things and of human affairs. Our neglect or failure to do some small thing may cause a long delay in getting what we want. Do, every day, all that can be done that day.

There is, however, a limitation or qualification of the above that we must take into account. We are not to overwork, nor to rush blindly into our business in the effort to do the greatest possible number of things in the shortest possible time.

We are not to try to do tomorrow's work today, nor to do a week's work in a day. It is really not the number of things we do, but the EFFICIENCY of each separate action that counts.

Every act is, in itself, either a success or a failure. Every act is either effective and efficient or ineffective and inefficient.

Every inefficient act is a failure. If we spend our life in doing inefficient acts, our whole life will be a failure. The more things we do, the worse for us if all our acts are inefficient ones.

On the other hand, every efficient act is a success in itself. If every act of our life is an efficient one, our whole life must be a success. The cause of failure is doing too many things in an inefficient manner and not doing enough things in an efficient manner.

You will see that it is a self-evident proposition that if you do not do any inefficient acts, and if you do a sufficient number of efficient acts, you will become rich. If, now, it is possible for you to make each act an efficient one, you will see again that the getting of riches is reduced to an exact science, like mathematics.

The matter turns, then, on the question of whether you can make each separate act a success in itself. And this you can certainly do. You can make each act a success, because ALL power is working with you. ALL power cannot fail.

Power is at your service, and to make each act efficient you have only to put power into it. Every action is either strong or weak. When every action is strong, you are acting in the certain way which will make you rich. Every act can be made strong and efficient by holding your vision while you are doing it and putting the whole power of FAITH and PURPOSE into it.

It is at this point that the people who separate mental power from personal action fail. They use the power of mind in one place and at one time, and they act in another way in another place and at another time. Their acts are not successful in themselves. Too many of them are inefficient. But if ALL power goes into every act, no matter how commonplace, every act will be a success in itself. Since it is the nature of things that every success opens the way to other successes, your progress towards what you want and the progress of what you want towards you, will become increasingly rapid.

Remember that successful action is cumulative in its results. Since the desire for more life is inherent in all things, when a person begins to move toward larger life, more things attach themselves to him, and the influence of his desire is multiplied.

Do, every day, all that you can do that day, and do each act in an efficient manner.

In saying that you must hold your vision while you are doing each act, however trivial or common-place, I do not mean to say that it is necessary at all times to see the vision distinctly to its smallest details. It should be the work of your leisure hours to use your imagination on the details of your vision and to contemplate them until they are firmly fixed upon memory. If you wish speedy results, spend practically all your spare time in this practice.

By continuous contemplation you will get the picture of what you want - even to the smallest details - so firmly fixed upon your mind and so completely transferred to the mind of formless substance, that in your working hours you need only to mentally refer to the picture to stimulate your faith and purpose and cause your best effort to be put forth.

Contemplate your picture in your leisure hours until your consciousness is so full of it that you can grasp it instantly. You will become so enthused with its bright promises that the mere thought of it will call forth the strongest energies of your whole being.

Let us again repeat our syllabus, and by slightly changing the closing statement bring it to the point we have now reached.

There is a thinking stuff from which all things are made, and which, in its original state, permeates, penetrates, and fills the interspaces of the universe.

A thought in this substance produces the thing that is imaged by the thought.

A person can form things in his thought, and, by impressing his thought upon formless substance, can cause the thing thought about to be created.

In order to do this, a person must pass from the competitive to the creative mind. He must form a clear mental picture of the things he wants, and must do - with faith and purpose - all that can be done each day, doing each separate thing in an efficient manner.

Chapter 13

Getting
in to the
Right Business

Success in any business, depends for one thing, upon your possessing in a well-developed state, the faculties required in that business. A music teacher can not succeed without good musical faculty. In any of the mechanical trades, without well-developed mechanical faculties no one can achieve great success. In mercantile pursuits, without tact and the commercial faculties no one can succeed.

Conversely, the faculties required in your particular vocation does not insure getting rich. There are musicians who have remarkable talent, and remain poor. There are blacksmiths, carpenters, and so on who have excellent mechanical ability, but who do not get rich. There are even merchants with good faculties for dealing with people who nevertheless fail.

The different faculties are tools. It is essential to have good tools. Furthermore, the tools should be used in the right way. One man can take a sharp saw, a square, a good plane, and so on, and build a handsome article of furniture. Another man can take the same tools and set to work to duplicate the article, but his production will be a botch. He does not know how to use good tools in a successful way.

The various faculties of your mind are the tools with which you must do the work which is to make you rich. So it will be easier for you to succeed if you get into a business for which you are well equipped with mental tools.

Generally speaking, you will do best in that business which will use your strongest faculties - the one for which you are naturally "best fit." There are limitations to this statement. No one should regard their vocation as being irrevocably fixed by the tendencies with which he was born.

You can get rich in any business, for if you have not the right talent, you can develop that talent. It merely means that you will have to make your tools as you go along, instead of confining yourself to the use of those with which you were born. It will be easier for you to succeed in a vocation for which you already have the talents in a well-developed state.

You can succeed in any vocation, for you can develop any rudimentary talent, and there is no talent of which you have not at least the rudiment.

You will get rich most easily in terms of effort, if you do that for which you are best fit, but you will get rich most satisfactorily if you do that which you want to do. Doing what you want to do is life. There is no real satisfaction in living if we are compelled to be forever doing something which we do not like to do, and can never do what we want to do. It is certain that we can do what we want to do.

The desire to do it is proof that you have within you the power which can do it. Desire is a manifestation of power. The desire to play music is the power which can play music seeking expression and development. The desire to invent mechanical devices is the mechanical talent seeking expression and development.

Where there is no power, either developed or undeveloped, to do a thing, there is never any desire to do that thing. Where there is strong desire to do a thing, it is certain proof that the power to do it is strong and only requires to be developed and applied in the right way.

All other things being equal, it is best to select the business for which you have the best developed talent. But if you have a strong desire to engage in any particular line of work, you should select that work as the ultimate end at which you aim.

You can do what you want to do. It is your right and privilege to follow the business or avocation which will be most congenial and pleasant. You are not obliged to do what you do not like to do, and should not do it except as a means to bring you to the doing of the thing you ultimately want to do.

If there are past mistakes whose consequences have placed you in an undesirable business or environment, you may be obliged for some time to do what you do not like to do. You can make the doing of it pleasant by knowing that it is making it possible for you to come to the doing of what you really want to do.

If you feel that you are not in the right vocation, do not act too hastily in trying to get into another one. The best way, generally, to change business or environment is by growth.

Do not be afraid to make a sudden and radical change if the opportunity is presented and you feel after careful consideration that it is the right opportunity. However, never take sudden or radical action when you are in doubt as to the wisdom of doing so.

There is never any hurry on the creative plane. There is no lack of opportunity. When you get out of the competitive mind you will understand that you never need to act hastily.

No one else is going to beat you to the thing you want to do. There is enough for all. If one space is taken, another and a better one will be opened for you a little farther on. There is plenty of time. When you are in doubt, wait. Fall back on the contemplation of your vision, and increase your faith and purpose. By all means, in times of doubt and indecision, cultivate gratitude. A day or two spent in contemplating the vision of what you desire and in earnest thanksgiving that you are getting it, will bring your mind into such close relationship with the Supreme that you will make no mistake when you do act.

There is a Mind which knows all there is to know. You can come into close unity with this Mind by faith and the purpose to advance in life, if you have deep gratitude.

Mistakes come from acting hastily or from acting in fear or doubt, or in forgetfulness of the right motive, which is more life to all, and less to none.

As you go on in the certain way, opportunities will come to you in increasing number, thus you will need to be very steady in your faith and purpose, and to keep in close touch with the Supreme Mind by reverent gratitude.

Do all that you can do in a perfect manner every day, but do it without haste, worry, or fear. Go as fast as you can, but never hurry.

Remember that in the moment you begin to hurry, you cease to be a creator and become a competitor, which would cause you to drop back upon the old plane again.

Whenever you find yourself hurrying, call a halt. Fix your attention on the mental image of the thing you want, and begin to give thanks that you are getting it. The exercise of GRATITUDE will never fail to strengthen your faith and renew your purpose.

Chapter 14

The

Impression of Increase

Whether you change your vocation or not, your actions for the present must be those pertaining to the business in which you are now engaged. You can get into the business you want by making constructive use of the business you are already established in by doing your daily work in the certain way.

Insofar as your business consists in dealing with other people, whether personally or by letter, the key thought of all your efforts must be to convey to their minds the impression of increase. Increase is what all men and all women are seeking. It is the urge of the Formless Intelligence within them seeking fuller expression.

The desire for increase is inherent in all nature. It is the fundamental impulse of the universe. All human activities are based on the desire for increase. People seek more food, more clothes, better shelter, more luxury, more beauty, more knowledge, more pleasure, more life. Every living thing is under this necessity for continuous advancement. Where increase of life ceases, dissolution and death set in at once.

Man instinctively knows this, and therefore is forever seeking more. This law of perpetual increase was set forth by Jesus in the parable of the talents. "Only those who gain more retain any; from him who has not shall be taken away even that which he has."

The normal desire for increased wealth is not an evil or a reprehensible thing. It is simply the desire for more abundant life. It is aspiration. And because it is the deepest instinct of their natures, all men and women are attracted to those who can give them more of the means of life.

In following the certain way as described in the foregoing pages, you are getting continuous increase for yourself, and you are giving it to all with whom you deal. You are a creative center from which increase is given off to all. Be sure of this, and convey assurance of the fact to every man, woman, and child with whom you come in contact. No matter how small the transaction, even if it be only the selling of a stick of candy to a little child, put into it the thought of increase. Make sure that the customer is impressed with the thought.

Convey the impression of advancement with everything you do, so that all people will receive the impression that you are an *advancing personality*, and that you advance all who deal with you. Convey the impression of advancement even to the people whom you meet in a social way - without any thought of business and to whom you do not try to sell anything. Give the thought of increase.

You can convey this impression of advancement by holding the unshakable faith that you, yourself, are in the way of increase by letting this faith inspire, fill, and permeate every action.

Do everything that you do in the firm conviction that you are an advancing personality and that you are giving advancement to everybody. Feel that you are getting rich, and that in so doing you are making others rich and conferring benefits on all.

Do not boast or brag of your success or talk about it unnecessarily. True faith is never boastful. Wherever you find a boastful person, you find one who is secretly doubtful and afraid. Simply feel the faith, and let it work out in every transaction. Let every act, tone and look express the quiet assurance that you are rich. Words will not be necessary to communicate this feeling to others. They will feel the sense of increase when in your presence, and will be attracted to you again.

You must so impress others that they will feel that in associating with you they will get increase for themselves. See that you give them a use value greater than the cash value you take from them.

Take an honest pride in doing this. Let everybody know it. You will have no lack of customers.

People will go where they are given increase. The Supreme, which desires increase in all and which knows all, will move towards you men and women who have never heard of you. Your business will increase rapidly. You will be surprised at the unexpected benefits which will come to you. You will be able from day to day to make larger combinations, secure greater advantages, and to go on into a more congenial vocation if you desire to do so. But in doing all this, you must never lose sight of the vision of what you want, or your faith and purpose to get what you want.

Let me here give you another word of caution in regard to motives. Beware of the insidious temptation to seek for power over other people.

Nothing is so pleasant to the unformed or partially developed mind as the exercise of power or dominion over others. The desire to rule for selfish gratification has been the curse of the world. For countless ages kings and lords have drenched the earth with blood in their battles to extend their dominions - not to seek more life for all, but to get more power for themselves.

Today, the main motive in the business and industrial world is the same. Men marshal their armies of dollars and lay waste the lives and hearts of millions in the same mad scramble for power over others.

Commercial kings, like political kings, are inspired by the lust for power. Vigilantly guard against any temptation to seek for authority, to become a master over others, or to impress others by lavish display.

The mind that seeks for mastery over others is the competitive mind, and the competitive mind is not the creative one. In order to master your environment and your destiny, it is not at all necessary that you should rule over others. Indeed, when you fall into the world's struggle for the high places, you begin to be conquered by fate and environment. Your getting rich becomes a matter of chance and speculation.

Beware of the competitive mind. No better statement of the principle of creative action can be formulated than the favorite declaration of the late "Golden Rule" Jones of Toledo who said, *"What I want for myself, I want for everybody."*

Chapter 15

The
Advancing Personality

What was said in the last chapter applies as much to the professional person as the hourly wage earner, or any other form of business. Whether a person be a physician, teacher, or clergyman, if that person can give increase of life to others and make them sensible of that fact, they will attract people. They will be rich.

The physician who holds the vision of being a great and successful healer, and who works toward the complete realization of that vision with faith and purpose, as described in former chapters, will come into such close touch with the source of life that he will be phenomenally successful. Patients will come to this physician in multitudes.

No one has a greater opportunity to carry into effect the teaching of this book than the practitioner of medicine. It does not matter to which of the various schools the practitioner may belong, for the principle of healing is common to all of them and may be reached by all alike. The *advancing person* in medicine, who holds to a clear mental image of being successful, and who obeys the laws of faith, purpose, and gratitude, will cure every curable case he undertakes.

In the field of religion, the world cries out for the clergyman who can inspire hearers to embrace the true science of abundant life. The person who masters the details of the science of getting rich, together with the allied sciences of being well, of being great, and of winning love, and teaches these details from the pulpit, will never lack for a congregation. This is a gospel that the world needs. It will give increase of life. People will hear it gladly and give liberal support to the person who brings it to them.

What is now needed is a demonstration of the science of life from the pulpit. We desire preachers who can not only tell us how, but who in their own persons will show us how. We need the preacher who will himself be rich, healthy, great, and beloved, to teach us how to attain to these things. When he comes, he will have a numerous and loyal following.

The same is true of the teacher who can inspire children with the faith and purpose of the advancing life. This teacher will never be out of a job. Any teacher who has this faith and purpose can give it to his or her pupils. He cannot help giving it to them if it is part of his own life and practice. What is true of the teacher, preacher, and physician is true of the lawyer, dentist, real estate agent, insurance agent and of everyone.

The combined mental and personal action described is infallible; it cannot fail. Every man and woman who follows these instructions steadily, perseveringly, and to the letter, will get rich. The law of the increase of life is as mathematically certain in its operation as the law of gravity. Getting rich is an exact science.

The wage-earner will find this as true of his case as of any of the others mentioned. Do not feel there is no chance to get rich because you work where there is no visible opportunity for advancement, where wages are small and the cost of living high. Form a clear mental vision of what you want and begin to act with faith and purpose.

Do all the work you can do, every day, and do each piece of work in a perfectly successful manner. Put the power of success and the purpose to get rich into everything you do. Do not do this merely with the idea of currying favor with an employer, in the hope that he, or those in place of authority, will see your good work and advance you. It is not likely they will do so.

The person who is merely a good worker, filling his place to the very best of his ability and satisfied with that, is valuable to that employer. It is not to the employer's interest to promote him. This worker is worth more where he is. Securing advancement requires something more than to be too large for your place.

The person who is certain to advance is the one who is too big for his current place. He has a clear concept of what he wants, knows he can become what he wants to be, and is determined to BE what he wants to be.

Do not try to do more than fill your present place with a view to pleasing your employer. Do it with the idea of advancing yourself. Hold the faith and purpose of increase during work hours, after work hours, and before work hours. Hold it in such a way that every person who comes in contact with you, whether foreman, fellow worker, or social acquaintance, will feel the power of purpose radiating from you. Let everyone get the sense of advancement and increase from you. People will be attracted to you. If there is no possibility for advancement in your present job, you will very soon see an opportunity to take another job.

There is a power which never fails to present opportunity to the advancing personality who is moving in obedience to law. God cannot help helping you if you act in a certain way. He must do so in order to help Himself.

There is nothing in your circumstances or in the industrial situation that can keep you down. If you cannot get rich working for a conglomerate, you can get rich running your own business. When you begin to move in the certain way, you will certainly escape from the clutches of the conglomerate and get your own business or wherever else you choose.

If a few thousand of its employees would enter upon the certain way, corporations would soon be in a bad plight. They would have to give their workers more opportunity or go out of business. Nobody has to work for a conglomerate.

Factories can keep people in so called hopeless conditions only so long as there are people who are ignorant of the science of getting rich or too intellectually slothful to practice it.

Begin this way of thinking and acting, and your faith and purpose will make you quick to see an opportunity to better your condition. Such opportunities will speedily come. The Supreme Power, working in all and working for you, will bring them to you.

Do not wait for an opportunity to be all that you want to be. When an opportunity to be more than you are now is presented and you feel impelled toward it, take it. It will be the first step toward a greater opportunity.

Know that there is no such thing possible in this universe as a lack of opportunities for the person who is living the advancing life. It is inherent in the constitution of the cosmos that all things shall be for you and work together for your good. You must certainly get rich if you act and think in the certain way. So let wage-earning men and women study this book with great care and enter with confidence upon the course of action it prescribes. It will not fail.

Chapter 16

Some Cautions
and
Concluding Observations

Some people may scoff at the idea that there is an exact science of getting rich. Holding to the impression that the supply of wealth is limited, they may insist that social and governmental institutions must be changed before even any considerable number of people can acquire a competence. But this is not true. It is true that existing governments keep the masses in poverty, but this is because the masses do not think and act in the certain way.

If the masses begin to move forward as suggested in this book, neither governments nor industrial systems can check them. All systems must be modified to accommodate the forward movement.

If people have the advancing mind, have the faith that they can become rich, and move forward with the fixed purpose to become rich, nothing can possibly keep anybody in poverty. Individuals may enter upon the certain way at any time and under any government and make themselves rich. When any considerable number of individuals do so under any government, the thoughts and actions will cause the system to be so modified as to open the way for others. The more people who get rich on the competitive plane, the worse for others. The more who get rich on the creative plane, the better for others.

The economic salvation of the masses can only be accomplished by getting a large number of people to practice the scientific method set down in this book and become rich. These will show others the way and inspire them with a desire for real life, with the faith that it can be attained, and with the purpose to attain it.

For the present, however, it is enough to know that neither the government under which you live, nor the capitalistic or competitive system of industry, can keep you from getting rich. When you enter upon the creative plane you will rise above all these things and become a citizen of another kingdom.

Remember, you must hold your thought upon the creative plane. You are never for an instant to be betrayed into regarding the supply as limited, or into acting on the moral level of competition. If you do fall into old ways of thought, correct yourself instantly. For when you are in the competitive mind, you have lost the cooperation of the Supreme Mind.

Do not spend any time in planning as to how you will meet possible emergencies in the future, except as the necessary policies may affect your actions today. You are concerned with doing today's work in a perfectly successful manner and not with emergencies which may arise tomorrow. You can attend to them as they come.

Do not concern yourself with questions as to how you will surmount obstacles which may loom upon your business horizon, unless you can see plainly that your course must be altered today in order to avoid them. No matter how tremendous an obstruction may appear at a distance, you will find that if you go on in the certain way it will disappear as you approach it, or that a way over, under, through, or around it will appear.

No possible combination of circumstances can defeat a man or woman who is proceeding to get rich along strictly scientific lines. No man or woman who obeys the law can fail to get rich, any more than one can multiply two by two and fail to get four.

Give no anxious thought to possible disasters, obstacles, panics, or unfavorable combinations of circumstances. There is time enough to meet such things when they present themselves before you in the immediate present, and you will find that every difficulty carries with it the wherewithal for its overcoming.

Guard your speech. Never speak of yourself, your affairs, or of anything else in a discouraged or discouraging way.

Never admit the possibility of failure or speak in a way that infers failure as a possibility. Never speak of the times as being hard, or of business conditions as being doubtful. Times may be hard and business doubtful for those who are on the competitive plane, but they can never be so for you.

You can create what you desire. You are above fear. When others are having hard times and poor business, you will find your greatest opportunities.

Train yourself to think, and look upon the world as a something which is becoming, and growing. Regard seeming evil as being only that which is undeveloped. Always speak in terms of advancement. To do otherwise is to deny your faith, and to deny your faith is to lose it.

Never allow yourself to feel disappointed. You may expect to have a certain thing at a certain time and not get it at that time. This could appear to you as failure. If you hold to your faith you will find that the failure is only an apparent.

Go on in the certain way. If you do not receive that thing, you will receive something so much better that you will see that the seeming failure was really a great success.

A student of this science had set his mind on making a certain business combination which seemed to him at the time to be very desirable. He worked for some weeks to bring it about. When the crucial time came, the thing failed in a perfectly inexplicable way. It was as if some unseen influence had been working secretly against him. But he was not disappointed. On the contrary, he thanked God that his desire had been overruled, and went steadily on with a grateful mind. In a few weeks an opportunity so much better came his way that he would not have made the first deal on any account. He saw that a mind which knew more had prevented him from losing the greater good by entangling himself with the lesser.

That is the way every seeming failure will work out for you. Keep your faith. Hold to your purpose. Have gratitude. Do every day all that can be done that day and do each separate act in a successful manner.

When you make a failure, it is because you have not asked for enough. Keep on, and a larger thing than you were seeking will certainly come to you. Remember this.

You will not fail because you lack the necessary talent to do what you wish to do. If you go on as directed, you will develop all the talent that is necessary to the doing of your work. It is not within the scope of this book to deal with the science of cultivating talent, but it is as certain and simple as the process of getting rich.

However, do not hesitate or waver for fear that when you come to any certain place you might fail for lack of ability. Keep right on, and when you come to that place, the ability will be furnished to you. The same source of ability which enabled the untaught Lincoln to do the greatest work in government ever accomplished by a single man, is open to you. You may draw upon all the mind there is for wisdom to use in meeting the responsibilities which are laid upon you.

Go on in full faith. Study this book. Make it your constant companion until you have mastered all the ideas contained in it. While you are getting firmly established in this faith, you will do well to give up most recreations and pleasures. Stay away from places where ideas conflicting with these are advanced in lectures or sermons. Do not read pessimistic or conflicting literature or get into arguments upon the matter.

Invest most of your leisure time in contemplating your vision, cultivating gratitude, and reading this book. It contains all you need to know of the science of getting rich. You will find all the essentials summed up in the next chapter.

Chapter 17

A Summary

of

the

Science of Getting Rich

There is a thinking stuff from which all things are made which, in its original state, permeates, penetrates, and fills the interspaces of the universe. A thought in this substance produces the thing that is imaged by the thought. A person can form things in thought, and by impressing thought upon formless substance can cause the thing thought about to be created.

In order to do this, a person must pass from the competitive to the creative mind. Otherwise the person cannot be in harmony with the formless intelligence, which is always creative and never competitive in spirit.

A person may come into full harmony with the formless substance by entertaining a lively and sincere gratitude for the blessings it bestows upon him. Gratitude unifies the mind of man with the intelligence of Substance, so that man's thoughts are received by the formless. A person can remain upon the creative plane only by uniting himself with the Formless Intelligence through a deep and continuous feeling of gratitude.

A person must form a clear and definite mental image of the things he desires to have, do, or become, and must hold this mental image, while being deeply grateful to the Supreme that all desires are granted. The person who wishes to get rich must spend his leisure hours in contemplating his vision, and in earnest thanksgiving that the reality is being given. Too much stress cannot be laid on the importance of frequent contemplation of the mental image, coupled with unwavering faith and devout gratitude. This is the process by which the impression is given to the formless and the creative forces set in motion.

The creative energy works through the established channels of natural growth, and of the industrial and social order. All that is included in his mental image will surely be brought to the person who follows the instructions given above, and whose faith does not waver. What he wants will come to him through the ways of established trade and commerce.

In order to receive his own when it is ready to come to him, he must be in action in a way that causes him to more than fill his present place. He must keep in mind the PURPOSE to get rich through realization of his mental image. He must do, every day, all that can be done that day, taking care to do each act in a successful manner. He must give to every person a use value in excess of the cash value he receives, so that each transaction makes for more life. He must hold the advancing thought so that the impression of increase will be communicated to all with whom he comes into contact.

The men and women who practice the foregoing instructions will certainly get rich. The riches they receive will be in exact proportion to the definiteness of their vision, the fixity of their purpose, the steadiness of their faith, and the depth of their gratitude.

FREE BONUS:

http://www.freewebs.com/millionairesguide

Printed in the United States
72071LV00008B/88